Belinda Jeffery's

barbecue
perfection
COOKING CLASS

barbecue *perfection*

HINKLER BOOKS

barbecue
perfection

Food Editor
Jody Vassallo

Creative Director
Sam Grimmer

Project Editor
Lara Morcombe

First published in 2004 by Hinkler Books Pty Ltd
17–23 Redwood Drive
Dingley, VIC 3172 Australia
www.hinklerbooks.com

Printed in 2004

Disclaimer: The nutritional information listed under each recipe does not include the nutrient content of garnishes or any accompaniments not listed in specific quantitites in the ingredient list. The nutritional information for each recipe is an estimate only, and may vary depending on the brand of ingredients used, and due to natural biological variations in the composition of natural foods such as meat, fish, fruit and vegetables. The nutritional information was calculated by using Foodworks dietary analysis software (Version 3, Xyris Software Pty Ltd, Highgate Hill, Queensland, Australia) based on the Australian food composition tables and food manufacturers' data. Where not specified, ingredients are always analyzed as average or medium, not small or large.

ISBN: 1 7412 1594 3
EAN: 9 781741 215410

Printed and bound in China.

contents

an introduction to barbecue cooking

A balmy summer's day, a few good friends, a glass of wine and the aroma of cooking food – there's nothing quite like a barbecue. It can be as simple as a few hot dogs served with crusty bread and a fresh green salad or as fancy as an outdoor dinner party serving seafood kebabs, marinated lamb cutlets, char-broiled vegetable stacks and whole pieces of meat. Whatever the occasion, this book has exciting recipes that will impress.

safety

A safe barbecue is a fun barbecue. Clear a space for your barbecue, away from any bush or combustible material. If you have a balcony or backyard, set up your barbecue in a corner and make sure not to push it up against a wall as the heat can burn nearby surfaces.

If using a gas barbecue with a drip tray, line the tray with sand to prevent dripping fat from igniting. If your barbecue does not have an automatic ignition, purchase long matches or a gas lighter. The utensils you use when cooking on a barbecue are important; barbecue shops sell long handled tongs that will make turning food easy.

If there are young children in the gathering, be sure to keep them well away from the cooking area. Brightly colored kettle/weber barbecues are often tempting for little fingers. Keep a close eye on the children, and don't leave a hot barbecue unsupervised.

Never pour flammable liquid onto a barbecue to start it or to increase the heat.

types of barbecues

There are many barbecues available on the market. The main varieties are fuel burning, and gas or electric.

fuel burning fixed barbecues:
Fixed barbecues are usually built to a simple design in backyards, parks and picnic grounds. They are constructed with bricks or cement and have a flat plate and char. A wood fire is built under the plates and left to burn until the coals are hot. The disadvantage: they can't be moved in bad weather.

kettle/weber barbecues:
Increasingly popular over the years, kettle/weber barbecues come in a variety of sizes and are perfect for people living in units. They are portable and can be taken on holidays or to a park. They cook as an open barbecue, a smoker or a kettle oven.

brazier: Braziers are simple, small and portable barbecues consisting of a box for fuel and a broiler for cooking. Some braziers have lids that help the food cook evenly.

gas or electric barbecues

Easy to use and ready at a moment's notice, gas or electric barbecues are the most popular barbecues. These barbecues use trays of volcanic rock, which are heated with either electricity or gas, and a flat plate and char grill above the rocks. Usually mounted into timber stands, they often come with hoods that allow for even cooking and protection from the elements.

source of heat

wood

Lighting a wood fire can be tricky on a windy day. It can also be difficult if the wood is slightly damp or green. Gather blends of kindling to start the fire and slowly increase the size of the pieces of wood as the fire gathers heat. Don't be tempted to start cooking over a raging fire. Allow the fire time to burn down until you are left with a nice bed of hot coals. By this time your barbecue plate will be heated and ready for you to cook. Remember to keep stoking the fire.

charcoal, heat beads and barbecue briquettes

Charcoal, heat beads or barbecue briquettes are a widely used source of fuel for kettle/weber barbecues or braziers. They are easy to use and produce a reliable, constant source of heat. They are available from supermarkets or barbecue shops. To light them you will need to use firelighters, which are usually sold beside the heatbeads in the supermarket. Firelighters should only be used to light the beads, and not to keep a fire going. No cooking should commence until the firelighters have finished burning as they have been soaked in kerosene and give off an unpleasant aroma that can easily permeate the food. Don't be heavy handed with firelighters. It's best to read the manufacturer's instructions but as a general guide, 2–3 firelighters will ignite roughly 20 beads. Allow the fire to burn until the beads turn white. This will take approximately 40 minutes. After handling the charcoal and firelighters, make sure you wash your hands before handling the food.

gas or electricity:
Gas barbecues are fuelled with either a gas bottle or connected to a gas main. Electric barbecues can be connected to an electricity supply. A dial at the front of the barbecue controls the temperature.

cooking

There are two ways of barbecuing food – direct and indirect. Direct heat cooks the food directly over the flame or coals. Indirect heat applies only to kettle/weber barbecues, which have an oven-style set up.

direct heat:
To cook with direct heat is very simple. Preheat the barbecue to moderate-high, oil the grill using a long-handled pastry brush and place one piece of food onto the barbecue. The food should sizzle once it hits the hotplate, if it doesn't, remove it and allow the barbecue to continue heating. Start by searing the food on the hottest part of the barbecue; this is often towards the back.

Once you have turned the food, move it to a more moderate heat and continue cooking; this will allow the food to cook evenly without burning. It is a good idea to have one part of an electric or gas barbecue turned down low, so you can keep cooked food warm whilst finishing off pieces of meat that take longer.

You can use the flat plate as you would an element on a stove – to reheat marinades in a saucepan, to stir-fry or even to make pancakes.

indirect heat:
Although cooking with indirect heat is slower than cooking with direct heat, it imparts a unique flavor into the food. Light the barbecue using heat beads and firelighters. Refer to the manufacturer's instructions for the quantity of beads, which will vary according to the size of the barbecue and the amount of food being cooked.

1 Remove the lid and slide open the vent at the bottom of the kettle.

2 Put the racks into position and place the heat beads and firelighters into the side baskets. Light and leave until the beads are covered with a fine ash. Do not add any food until the beads are white. Do not cover the barbecue until the beads are heated.

3 Place a dish in the bottom of the kettle/weber to catch any excess fat. Position the cooking rack and top with the food. Cover and cook according to the recipe.

You can also use a kettle/weber as a smoker or oven and they are wonderful for roasting large pieces of meat or cooking the holiday ham or turkey. To smoke foods on a kettle, simply prepare the kettle as instructed above and when the heat beads are covered in white ash add a handful of smoking chips that have been soaked in water or wine for 30 minutes. Cover and smoke following the recipe.

meat

lamb chops with garlic mayonnaise

ingredients

$^1/_2$ cup (125 ml, 4 fl oz) olive oil
2 garlic cloves, minced
2 tablespoons finely chopped parsley
1 tablespoon chopped fresh thyme
1$^1/_2$ tablespoons lemon juice
12 rib lamb chops, each
    about $^1/_2$ inch thick
salt and freshly ground black pepper
quick aïoli
1 egg
$^3/_4$ cup (185 g, 6 oz) mayonnaise
1 tablespoon extra virgin olive oil
4 cloves garlic, minced
1 tablespoon lemon juice
serves 4

1 In a large shallow bowl, combine $^1/_2$ cup (125 ml, 4 fl oz) oil, 2 cloves garlic, parsley, thyme, and 1$^1/_2$ tablespoons lemon juice. Add chops and coat well. Cover and refrigerate for at least 2 hours.

2 Preheat barbecue to high heat. In a small bowl, combine egg, mayonnaise and remaining oil, lemon juice and garlic. Whisk until smooth.

3 Drain chops, reserving marinade. Cook the chops on barbecue for 2–3 minutes each side, basting occasionally with marinade. Season with salt and pepper. Serve drizzled with aïoli.

i

preparation time
30 minutes,
plus 2 hours
marinating

cooking time
20 minutes

nutritional value
fat: 24.8 g
carbohydrate: 4.2 g
protein: 12.4 g

greek shish kebabs

ingredients

750 g (1½ lb) lamb neck fillet,
   cut into 1 inch pieces
fresh mint to garnish
lemon wedges to serve

marinade
100 g (3½ oz) greek yogurt
½ onion, grated
2 cloves garlic, minced
juice of ½ lemon
1 tablespoon olive oil
3 tablespoons chopped fresh mint
salt and black pepper
8 small metal skewers

makes 8

preparation time
20 minutes

cooking time
15-20 minutes,
plus overnight
or 4 hours
marinating

nutritional value
fat: 5.5 g
carbohydrate: 1.5 g
protein: 16.8 g

1 Preheat barbecue to a high heat.

2 In a large bowl, combine yogurt, onion, garlic, lemon juice, oil, mint and seasoning. Add lamb and toss to coat. Cover and refrigerate for 4 hours or overnight.

3 Thread lamb onto metal skewers. Cook kebabs on barbecue for 10–12 minutes, turning 2–3 times, until cooked through. Garnish with mint and serve with lemon wedges.

1 To make marinade: place mint, garlic, yogurt, mustard and mint sauce in a large glass bowl and mix to combine. Add lamb, turn to coat, cover and refrigerate for 3 hours.

2 Preheat barbecue to a medium heat. For honeyed onions: heat oil on barbecue plate, add onions and cook, stirring constantly, for 10 minutes. Add honey and vinegar and cook, stirring, for a further 5 minutes or until onions are soft and golden.

3 Drain lamb, place on lightly oiled barbecue and cook for 2–3 minutes each side. Serve topped with onions.

lamb with honeyed onions

ingredients

12 lamb cutlets, trimmed of fat
yogurt marinade
1 tablespoon chopped fresh mint
1 clove garlic, minced
200 g (7 oz) natural yogurt
2 tablespoons wholegrain mustard
1 tablespoon mint sauce
honeyed onions
2 tablespoons olive oil
2 red onions, sliced
1 tablespoon honey
2 tablespoons red-wine vinegar
serves 4-6

i

preparation time
20 minutes, plus 3 hours marinating

cooking time
25 minutes

nutritional value
fat: 8.5 g
carbohydrate: 4.7 g
protein: 11.9 g

steaks with blue butter

and roll into a log shape. Refrigerate for 1 hour or until firm.

3 In a small bowl, place pepper and oil and mix to combine. Brush steaks lightly with oil mixture. Place steaks

on lightly oiled barbecue plate and cook for 3–5 minutes each side.

4 Cut butter into ½ inch-thick slices and top each steak with 1 or 2 slices. Serve immediately.

i

preparation time
20 minutes,
plus 1 hour
refrigeration

cooking time
15 minutes

nutritional value
fat: 23.4 g
carbohydrate: 0.4 g
protein: 16.5 g

ingredients

1 tablespoon freshly ground black pepper
2 tablespoons olive oil
6 fillet steaks, trimmed of fat
blue butter
125 g (4 oz) butter, softened
60 g (2 oz) blue cheese
1 tablespoon chopped parsley
1 teaspoon paprika
serves 6

1 Preheat barbecue plate to high.

2 In a small bowl, place butter, blue cheese, parsley and paprika and beat until well combined. Place blue butter on a piece of plastic food wrap

standing rib roast with cajun potato cakes and chunky salsa

ingredients

1.5 kg (3 lb) standing rib roast of beef
salt and pepper
2 cloves garlic, minced
2 tablespoons all purpose flour
300 g (10 oz) jar tomato salsa

cajun potato cakes

4 medium potatoes, boiled in jackets
2 eggs, lightly beaten
2 teaspoons cajun seasoning
2 tablespoons olive oil
2 tablespoons all purpose flour
$1/2$ teaspoon salt

serves 8

3 Dust roast with flour to seal in juices and place on barbecue. Cook roast in barbecue following instructions for cooking with indirect heat on page 7 for $1^{1}/_{2}$–2 hours.

4 Cook patties on oiled hotplate or grill bars over direct heat for about 5 minutes each side. Heat salsa while patties are cooking. Carve roast and serve with the cajun potato cakes and salsa.

1 Preheat hooded barbecue to a 180°C (350°F, gas mark 4) medium-high heat. Rub roast with salt, pepper and minced garlic and stand at room temperature for 20 minutes.

preparation time
20 minutes

cooking time
$1^{1}/_{2}$-2 hours, plus 20 minutes standing

nutritional value
fat: 5.4 g
carbohydrate: 5.1 g
protein: 13.2 g

2 Skin potatoes and mash well. Add eggs, cajun seasoning, olive oil, flour and salt. Mix well and form into 16 patties with floured hands.

lamb and salsa pockets

ingredients

¹/₂ leg of lamb, trimmed of fat
1 tablespoon lemon juice
salt and pepper
2 teaspoons oil
1 clove garlic, minced
bamboo skewers
300 g (10 oz) tomato salsa, warmed
6 pitta bread rounds
1 small lettuce, shredded

serves 6

i

preparation time
20 minutes, plus
20 minutes
marinating

cooking time
10 minutes

nutritional value
fat: 3.4 g
carbohydrate: 14.2 g
protein: 11.4 g

1 Preheat barbecue to a high heat. Soak bamboo skewers in warm water for 15 minutes. Cut lamb into ¹/₃ inch cubes. In a large glass bowl, place lamb, lemon juice, salt, pepper, oil and garlic. Cover and marinate at room temperature for 20 minutes. Thread onto skewers.

2 Lightly oil barbecue plate and cook lamb skewers for 3–4 minutes each side. Remove skewers.

3 Halve the pocket bread and heat a little on the barbecue. Open the pocket, fill with lettuce, lamb and top with heated salsa.

cajun cutlets

ingredients

125 g (4 oz) butter
3 teaspoons cajun seasoning
1 small red chilli pepper, deseeded
   and chopped
12 lamb cutlets, trimmed of fat
1 tablespoon olive oil
serves 4-6

1 Beat the butter to soften and mix in 1¹⁄₂ teaspoons of the cajun seasoning and the chilli pepper. Place butter in the center of a piece of plastic wrap or wax paper. Roll up into a thin sausage shape and twist at the ends. Refrigerate until firm.

2 Snip the membrane at the side of each cutlet to prevent curling. Flatten slightly with the side of a meat mallet. Combine the remaining cajun seasoning and the olive oil and rub into the cutlets. Place in a single layer onto a large pan, cover and stand for 20 minutes at room temperature, or overnight in the refrigerator.

3 Preheat barbecue to high. Place a sheet of baking paper on the grill bars, making a few slashes between the bars for ventilation. Place cutlets on grill and cook for 3–4 minutes each side. Serve topped with a slice of cajun butter on each cutlet.

i

preparation time
20 minutes, plus
20 minutes or
overnight
marinating

cooking time
15 minutes

nutritional value
fat: 24.5 g
carbohydrate: 0.2 g
protein: 16.6 g

mini lamb roast with barbecued noodles

ingredients

1 trim lamb mini roast
2 tablespoons chopped cilantro
1 clove garlic, minced
salt and pepper
1 tablespoon lemon juice
1 tablespoon oil

barbecued noodles
500 g (1 lb) hokkien noodles
1 tablespoon chopped cilantro
100 g (3½ oz) feta cheese, crumbled
1 clove garlic, minced
½ teaspoon chopped chilli
    pepper (optional)

serves 4

preparation time
20 minutes, plus
1 hour marinating

cooking time
1½ hours, plus 15
minutes standing

nutritional value
fat: 5.0 g
carbohydrate: 15.8 g
protein: 16.4 g

1 Preheat kettle/weber or hooded gas barbecue for indirect cooking. Tie the mini roast with kitchen string to retain moisture.

2 In a large glass bowl, combine cilantro, garlic, salt and pepper, lemon juice and oil. Place lamb into marinade and turn to coat on all sides. Marinate for 1 hour at room temperature.

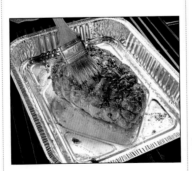

3 Place lamb over drip pan in center of barbecue, cover with lid or hood and cook for 35–40 minutes. There is no need to turn. Alternatively, place lamb in a foil pan, brushing with marinade as it cooks. Allow to stand 10–15 minutes before carving.

barbecued noodles:

1 Rinse noodles in hot water and separate. Drain well. In a small bowl combine cilantro, feta, garlic and chilli pepper, mixing to a paste.

2 Heat barbecue plate to high. Lightly oil and add noodles, tossing with cilantro paste. Mix well and heat through. (Alternatively use a baking pan on grill plate to cook noodles.)

3 Serve calved lamb on barbecued noodles and drizzle with remaining juices if desired.

barbecued lamb pitta breads

ingredients

1 tablespoon lemon finely grated zest
1 teaspoon ground cumin
1 tablespoon olive oil
750 g (1½ lb) lamb fillets
6 pitta bread rounds
125 g (4 oz) ready-made hummus
1 bunch endive (curly chicory)
250 g (8 oz) ready-made tabbouleh

serves 6

i

preparation time
15 minutes,
plus 30 minutes
marinating

cooking time
15 minutes

nutritional value
fat: 3.9 g
carbohydrate: 18.8 g
protein: 11.7 g

1 Combine lemon zest, cumin and oil in a small bowl. Rub surface of lamb with oil mixture place in a shallow glass dish and marinate at room temperature for 30 minutes.

2 Preheat barbecue to a medium heat. Place lamb on lightly oiled barbecue grill and cook for 3–5 minutes each side or until lamb is tender and cooked to your liking. Stand for 2 minutes before slicing.

3 Warm pitta breads on barbecue for 1–2 minutes each side. Split each pitta bread to make a pocket, then spread with hummus and fill with endive, tabbouleh and sliced lamb.

glazed pork spare ribs

ingredients

1 kg (2 lb) pork spare ribs
soy and honey marinade
4 tablespoons soy sauce
2 tablespoons honey
1 tablespoon sherry
2 cloves garlic, minced
1 teaspoon grated fresh ginger
serves 4

1 In a small bowl, combine all marinade ingredients. Place spare ribs on a large sheet of heavy-duty foil and cover both sides generously with marinade. Wrap into a double-folded parcel, making sure all joins are well sealed to prevent leakage. Stand for at least half an hour before cooking.

2 Prepare the barbecue for direct-heat cooking. Place a wire cake-rack on the grill bars to stand 1 inch above the bars. Place ribs in the foil parcel on the rack and cook for 10 minutes each side.

3 Remove to a plate, remove ribs and discard foil, then return ribs to rack. Continue cooking for about 10 minutes, brushing with fresh sauce or marinade and turning each minute until ribs are well browned and crisp.

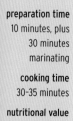

preparation time
10 minutes, plus
30 minutes
marinating

cooking time
30-35 minutes

nutritional value
fat: 6.2 g
carbohydrate: 5.2 g
protein: 25.3 g

honey- glazed thick straight hot dogs

Ingredients

2 kg (4 lb) thick pork or beef hot dogs
20 metal skewers
honey and chilli marinade
4 tablespoons red wine
1/2 cup (125 ml, 4 fl oz) honey
1/4 teaspoon ground chilli
1 teaspoon mustard powder
serves 4-8

1 Straighten each hot dog and thread carefully onto skewers through the center of the hot dog. For honey chilli marinade: In a small bowl, combine red wine, honey, chilli and mustard powder and set aside.

i

preparation time
5 minutes

cooking time
30-35 minutes

nutritional value
fat: 22.5 g
carbohydrate: 8.3 g
protein: 10.3 g

2 Heat barbecue to medium-high for indirect heat and medium for direct heat. Cook the hot dogs on a lightly oiled preheated barbecue grill or flat

plate, rolling the hot dogs back and forth until there is a color change. This gradually expands the skins and stops the casing from splitting.

3 If cooking on a flat-top gas barbecue or an electric barbecue grill, place a sheet of baking paper under hot dogs, brush with marinade and turn frequently. (A kettle/weber can be used.) Cook for 20–25 minutes until well glazed and cooked through. Remove skewers just before serving.

honey and sage pork chops

ingredients

6 loin pork chops
honey sage marinade
1 cup (250 ml, 8 fl oz) dry white wine
170 g (5½ oz) honey
1 tablespoon finely chopped fresh sage
serves 6

1 In a large glass bowl place wine, honey and sage and mix to combine. Add chops. Cover and marinate at room temperature for 2–3 hours, or overnight in the refrigerator.

2 Preheat barbecue to a medium heat. Drain chops and cook on lightly oiled barbecue for 5–6 minutes each side or until cooked.

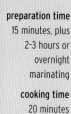

preparation time
15 minutes, plus
2-3 hours or
overnight
marinating

cooking time
20 minutes

nutritional value
fat: 2.8 g
carbohydrate: 11.2 g
protein: 13.8 g

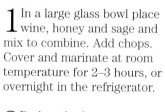

herbed and spiced pork loin

2 Rub marinade over pork, place in a large glass dish, cover and refrigerate overnight.

ingredients

2 kg (4 lb) boneless pork loin, rolled and
   rind scored at 1/2 inch intervals
herb and spice marinade
1 onion, chopped
2 tablespoons pink peppercorns, crushed
2 tablespoons crushed green peppercorns
2 tablespoons ground cilantro
1 tablespoon freshly ground black pepper
1 tablespoon ground cumin
1 teaspoon garam masala
1 teaspoon ground mixed spice
1 teaspoon turmeric
1 teaspoon paprika
1 teaspoon sea salt
2 tablespoons peanut oil
2 tablespoons sesame oil
1 tablespoon white vinegar
serves 8

preparation time
30 minutes, plus
overnight
marinating

cooking time
1 1/2 hours, plus 15
minutes standing

nutritional value
fat: 9.1 g
carbohydrate: 0.4 g
protein: 25.9 g

1 In a food processor or blender, place onion, peppercorns, cilantro, black pepper, cumin, garam masala, mixed spice, turmeric, paprika, salt, peanut oil, sesame oil and vinegar and process to a smooth paste.

Place pork on a wire rack set in a baking pan and bake at 190°C (375°F, gas mark 5) for 1 hour.

4 Preheat barbecue to a medium heat. Transfer pork to lightly oiled barbecue grill and cook, turning frequently, for 1 1/2 hours or until pork is tender and cooked through. Stand for 15 minutes before carving and serving.

2 Preheat barbecue to a medium heat. Thread 2 onion quarters onto six lightly oiled skewers, then brush with oil. Cook on lightly oiled barbecue, turning halfway through cooking, for 15–20 minutes or until onions are golden and tender.

3 Thread 2 potatoes onto another six lightly oiled skewers, then brush with oil. Cook on barbecue, turning halfway through cooking, for 10–15 minutes or until potatoes are golden and heated through.

4 Cook hot dogs on lightly oiled barbecue for 10–15 minutes or until they are golden and crisp on the outside and heated through.

mixed hot dog and onion grill

ingredients

12 assorted hot dogs
12 baby new potatoes, scrubbed and cooked
3 red onions, quartered
olive oil
12 metal skewers

serves 4-6

1 Parboil hot dogs by placing in a large pan, and covering with water. Bring slowly to the boil, reduce heat and simmer for 5 minutes. Drain, cool and refrigerate for several hours or overnight.

i

preparation time
20 minutes, plus
2-3 hours or
overnight
refrigeration

cooking time
30 minutes

nutritional value
fat: 15.2 g
carbohydrate: 7.4 g
protein: 5.5 g

perfect
t-bone
steak

ingredients

4 t-bone steaks
2 cloves of garlic, minced
2 teaspoons oil
salt and pepper

garlic butter

4 tablespoons butter
1 clove garlic, minced
1 tablespoon parsley flakes
2 teaspoons lemon juice

serves 4

2 Sear steaks for one minute each side. Cook for 2–3 minutes each side until cooked to your liking. Total time 5–6 minutes for rare, 7–10 minutes for medium and 10–14 minutes for well done.

3 Serve with garlic butter.

1 Preheat barbecue to a high heat. Bring the steaks to room temperature. Combine garlic, oil and salt and pepper. Rub onto both sides of steak. Stand for 10–15 minutes at room temperature.

cheese-filled beef patties

ingredients

600 g (1¼ lb) lean minced beef
1 tablespoon barbecue sauce
2 tablespoons tomato sauce
1 small onion, finely chopped
60 g (2 oz) mature cheddar, grated
125 g (4 oz) can crushed pineapple,
  drained
makes 4 large patties

i

preparation time
15 minutes

cooking time
30 minutes

nutritional value
fat: 7.1 g
carbohydrate: 3.9 g
protein: 15.9 g

1 Preheat barbecue to a medium heat. In a large bowl, place beef, barbecue sauce, tomato sauce and onion and mix to combine. Shape beef mixture into eight patties, flattening slightly with the palm of your hand.

2 Top 4 patties with cheese and pineapple, then cover with remaining patties, carefully moulding edges of patties together to form 4 larger patties.

3 Cook patties on lightly oiled barbecue for 10 minutes each side.

slow-roasted leg of lamb

ingredients

1.5 kg (3 lb) leg of lamb
3 cloves garlic, thinly sliced
herb marinade
4 tablespoons chopped fresh rosemary
4 tablespoons chopped fresh mint
1/2 cup (125 ml, 4 fl oz) white wine vinegar
4 tablespoons olive oil
freshly ground black pepper
serves 6-8

1 In a small bowl, place rosemary, mint, vinegar, oil and black pepper and mix to combine. Set aside.

2 Cut several deep slits in the surface of the lamb. Fill each slit with a slice of garlic. Place lamb in a large glass dish, pour over marinade, turn to coat, cover and refrigerate for 4 hours.

3 Preheat hooded barbecue to medium. (A kettle/weber can also be used. See instructions page 7.) Place lamb on a wire cake rack set in a roasting pan and pour over marinade. Place roasting pan on rack in barbecue, cover barbecue with lid and cook, basting occasionally, for 1 1/2–2 hours or until lamb is tender. Cover and stand for 15 minutes before carving.

i

preparation time
20 minutes, plus
4 hours marinating

cooking time
1 1/2 hours, plus 15
minutes standing

nutritional value
fat: 9.5 g
carbohydrate: 0.1 g
protein: 19.1 g

spiced beef and carrot burgers

ingredients

500 g (1 lb) lean minced beef
2 carrots, coarsely grated
90 g (3 oz) mushrooms, finely chopped
1 large onion, finely chopped
90 g (3 oz) fresh whole-wheat
   breadcrumbs
2 tablespoons tomato paste
1 egg, lightly beaten
1 clove garlic, minced
2 teaspoons ground cumin
2 teaspoons ground cilantro
1 teaspoon hot chilli powder
black pepper
serves 4

1 Preheat barbecue to a medium heat. In a large bowl, place all the ingredients and mix to combine.

2 Shape the mixture into 4 round flat burgers, using your hands. Cook on barbecue for 10–15 minutes, until lightly browned, turning once. Serve with toasted buns, lettuce, tomato and a tangy relish.

i

preparation time
25 minutes

cooking time
20 minutes

nutritional value
fat: 4.1 g
carbohydrate: 8.0 g
protein: 12.1 g

chicken

1 Preheat barbecue to high. In a small pan, combine cranberry sauce, tomato sauce, brown sugar, vinegar, mustard and garlic powder. Bring to the boil, reduce heat and simmer, uncovered, for 5 minutes, stirring occasionally.

cranberry-grilled chicken quarters

ingredients

½ cup (125 g, 4 oz) cranberry sauce
4 tablespoons tomato sauce
1 tablespoon light brown sugar
1 tablespoon vinegar
1 tablespoon mustard
¼ teaspoon garlic powder
1 x 1.5 kg (3 lb) boiling chicken, quartered
rice pilaf (optional)
parsley (optional)
serves 4

i

preparation time
25 minutes

cooking time
1 hour

nutritional value
fat: 8.4 g
carbohydrate: 4.7 g
protein: 16.2 g

2 Break the wing, hip and drumstick joints so chicken pieces lie flat. Barbecue chicken, skin side down, over direct heat for 20 minutes. Turn chicken, grill for a further 20–30 minutes or until chicken is tender, brushing occasionally with sauce. (It can be cooked in a kettle/weber for 50–60 minutes.) Heat any remaining sauce until bubbly. Serve chicken with sauce and, if using, rice pilaf and parsley.

grilled spring equinox chicken salad

ingredients

1/2 bunch fresh cilantro
3 tablespoons olive oil
1 tablespoon lime juice
1 tablespoon ground cumin
1 tablespoon grated fresh ginger
3 cloves garlic, minced
1/4 teaspoon paprika
1/4 teaspoon salt
1/2 cup (125 ml, 4 fl oz) dry vermouth
6 (about 750 g, 11/2 lb) chicken breast
    fillet halves
3 cups (550 g, 11/4 lb) cooked brown
    basmati rice
1 red bell pepper
1 green bell pepper
1 yellow or orange bell pepper
1 bunch english spinach, cut into strips
425 g (14 oz) can pinto beans, rinsed
    and drained
125 g (4 oz) can corn kernels, drained
1/2 cup (125 ml, 4 fl oz) sour cream
4 green onions, sliced
serves 6

preparation time
30 minutes, plus
30 minutes or 2
hours marinating

cooking time
10 minutes

nutritional value
fat: 6.0 g
carbohydrate: 19.2 g
protein: 9.5 g

1 In a blender or food processor, place cilantro, oil, lime juice, cumin, ginger, garlic, paprika and salt. Blend or process until nearly smooth and set aside.

2 In a large glass bowl, combine vermouth and 3 tablespoons of the sauce. Place chicken in bowl, turn to coat chicken. Cover and marinate at room temperature for 30 minutes or in the refrigerator for 2 hours.

3 Seed and quarter the bell peppers, set aside. Prepare charcoal or gas barbecue grill for medium heat. Remove chicken from marinade, reserve marinade. Cook chicken on barbecue grill for 12–15 minutes or until tender,

brushing once with reserved marinade. Discard remaining marinade. Lightly brush bell pepper with 1 tablespoon olive oil. Place bell pepper on the barbecue grill and cook for 8–10 minutes or until tender, turning occasionally. Remove bell pepper and chicken from barbecue and slice into 1/3 inch strips.

4 To serve, mound 1/2 cup cooked rice in the center of six serving plates. Surround rice with some spinach. Divide grilled chicken, bell pepper, pinto beans and corn among the plates. In a small bowl, combine remaining sauce and sour cream and drizzle over each salad. Garnish with green onions.

warm thai chicken salad

ingredients

4 chicken breast fillets
2 teaspoons ready-made thai-style
   marinade
1 teaspoon oil
1 red bell pepper, deseeded and
   cut into strips
1 green bell pepper, deseeded and
   cut into strips
1 eggplant, sliced
1 spanish onion, cut into rings
1/2 cos (romaine) lettuce, shredded

dressing

1/2 cup (125 ml, 4 fl oz) olive oil
4 tablespoons malt vinegar
extra teaspoon ready-made thai-style
   marinade

serves 4

1 Flatten chicken breasts slightly to even thickness. In a small bowl, combine 2 teaspoons thai-style marinade

and 1 teaspoon oil and rub well into the chicken. Cover and stand 20 minutes before cooking.

2 Heat the barbecue to medium-high and lightly oil hotplate and grill bars. Place chicken on grill and cook 4 minutes each side. Place bell peppers, eggplant and onion on the hotplate, drizzle with a little oil and cook for 5–8 minutes, tossing to cook through. Pile lettuce onto individual plates and place barbecued vegetables in the center. Cut the chicken into thin diagonal slices and arrange on top of vegetables.

3 In a small bowl, combine vinegar and remaining oil and thai-style marinade and pour over chicken and warm salad. Serve with crusty bread.

i

preparation time
15 minutes, plus
20 minutes
standing

cooking time
15 minutes

nutritional value
fat: 8.9 g
carbohydrate: 0.9 g
protein: 13.8 g

cranberry chicken skewers

ingredients

750 g (1½ lb) minced chicken
30 g (1 oz) breadcrumbs
1 onion, chopped
2 cloves garlic, minced
2 tablespoons chopped fresh sage
1 teaspoon mixed spice
10-12 metal skewers
1 egg, lightly beaten
¼ teaspoon tabasco sauce
½ cup (125 ml, 4 fl oz) cranberry sauce,
   warmed

serves 6

i

preparation time
20 minutes, plus
2 hours
refrigeration

cooking time
5-10 minutes

nutritional value
fat: 6.3 g
carbohydrate: 7.9 g
protein: 14.6 g

1 In a large bowl, place chicken, breadcrumbs, onion, garlic, sage, mixed spice, egg and tabasco sauce and mix to combine.

2 Shape chicken mixture around lightly oiled metal skewers to form 3 inch sausage shapes. Cover and refrigerate for 2 hours.

3 Preheat barbecue to a medium heat. Place skewers on lightly oiled barbecue grill and cook, turning several times, for 5–10 minutes or until skewers are cooked. Drizzle with cranberry sauce and serve.

buffalo chilli chicken

ingredients

1 kg (2 lb) chicken pieces, skinned
3 green onions, chopped
2 cloves garlic, minced
1 cup (250 ml, 8 fl oz) tomato sauce
4 tablespoons beer
1 tablespoon cider vinegar
1 tablespoon honey
1 tablespoon tabasco sauce
serves 4-6

1 Score larger pieces of chicken at 1/2 inch intervals and set aside.

2 Place green onions, garlic, tomato sauce, beer, vinegar, honey and tabasco sauce in a large shallow glass dish and mix to combine. Add chicken, toss to coat, cover and refrigerate for 3–4 hours.

3 Preheat barbecue to a medium heat. Drain chicken and reserve marinade. Place chicken on lightly oiled barbecue grill and cook, basting frequently with reserved marinade and turning several times, for 10–15 minutes or until chicken is tender and cooked through.

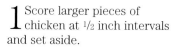

i

preparation time
20 minutes, plus
3-4 hours
marination

cooking time
10-15 minutes

nutritional value
fat: 5.5 g
carbohydrate: 6.5 g
protein: 13.5 g

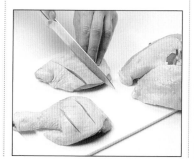

chicken patties served on basil flapjacks with chilli yogurt sauce

1 In a large bowl, combine all patty ingredients, mixing well with hands. Cover and refrigerate for 20 minutes. With wet hands, form into small flat patties about 1 inch in diameter. Place on a baking sheet, cover and refrigerate.

greased hotplate. Cook until bubbles appear over the surface and the bottom is golden. Flip over with a spatula and cook until golden. Transfer to a clean towel and cover to keep hot. Cook patties for 8–10 minutes until golden.

ingredients

patties
500 g (1 lb) minced chicken
$^1/_2$ teaspoon salt
$^1/_4$ teaspoon pepper
1 clove garlic, minced
$^1/_2$ teaspoon chopped fresh chilli pepper
2 tablespoons dried breadcrumbs
4 tablespoons water

flapjacks
150 g (5 oz) cake flour
$^1/_4$ teaspoon salt
2 tablespoons chopped fresh basil
1 clove garlic, minced
$^3/_4$ cup (185 ml, 6 fl oz) milk
1 egg

chilli yogurt sauce
200 g (7 oz) natural yogurt
2 teaspoons sweet chilli sauce

serves 6

4 In a small bowl, combine yogurt and sweet chilli sauce. Serve flapjacks topped with 3 patties and a dollop of chilli yogurt sauce.

2 For the flapjacks, sift the flour and salt into a large bowl. In a separate bowl, combine the basil, garlic and milk, then beat in the egg. Make a well in the center of the flour and pour in the milk mixture. Stir to form a smooth batter. Cover and set aside for 20 minutes.

3 Heat barbecue until hot and lightly oil the grill bars and hotplate. Brush the patties with a little oil and place on grill bars. Grill for 2 minutes each side. Pour 4 tablespoons of flapjack mixture onto the

i

preparation time
30 minutes

cooking time
30 minutes

nutritional value
fat: 5.5 g
carbohydrate: 12.3 g
protein: 11.9 g

chilli lime legs

ingredients

4 tablespoons lime juice
4 tablespoons buttermilk
2 tablespoons sweet chilli sauce
2 tablespoons soy sauce
12 chicken drumsticks, skinned
serves 4-6

i

preparation time
10 minutes, plus 3 hours marinating

cooking time
25 minutes

nutritional value
fat: 9.9 g
carbohydrate: 0.6 g
protein: 15.8 g

1 In a large shallow glass dish, place lime juice, buttermilk, sweet chilli sauce and soy sauce and mix to combine. Score each drumstick in several places, add to lime juice mixture, turn to coat, cover and refrigerate for 3 hours.

2 Preheat barbecue to a medium heat. Drain chicken well and reserve marinade. Place chicken on lightly oiled barbecue grill and cook, basting frequently with reserved marinade and turning occasionally, for 25 minutes or until chicken is cooked.

mustard and honey chicken drumsticks with mustard cream sauce

ingredients

2.25 kg (4.5 lb) chicken drumsticks
mustard cream sauce
1¼ cups (315 ml, 10 fl oz) sour cream
1 cup (250 ml, 8 fl oz) dijon mustard
½ cup (125 ml, 4 fl oz) honey and chilli marinade
honey and chili marinade
¾ cup (185 ml, 6 fl oz) red wine
1½ cups (375 ml, 12 fl oz) honey
¾ teaspoon ground chilli
3 teaspoons mustard powder
serves 6-10

1 In a large bowl, combine red wine, honey, chilli and mustard powder. Set aside and reserve ½ cup (125 ml, 4 fl oz) marinade in a separate bowl. Place drumsticks in a large glass dish and pour over 1¾ cups (435 ml, 14 fl oz) marinade. Cover and stand 30 minutes at room temperature or overnight in the refrigerator.

2 Heat a flat-top, charcoal or gas barbecue until hot. Lightly oil grill bars, place drumsticks on barbecue and cook for 30–35 minutes or until golden and cooked through to the bone. Brush frequently with marinade and turn drumsticks to brown evenly. (It can be cooked in a kettle/weber for 40–45 minutes.)

3 In a heat-proof bowl, combine sour cream, mustard, and remaining ½ cup (125 ml, 4 fl oz) honey and chilli marinade. Place at the side of the barbecue to heat through. Serve drumsticks with the mustard cream sauce and vegetable accompaniments or salad.

i

preparation time
30 minutes

cooking time
35-45 minutes

nutritional value
fat: 10.9 g
carbohydrate: 13.3 g
protein: 11.9 g

spicy mango chicken

ingredients

4 chicken breast fillets
1 teaspoon freshly ground black pepper
1 teaspoon ground cumin
1 teaspoon paprika
4 slices prosciutto or ham, halved
2 mangoes, peeled and cut into ½ inch thick slices

mango sauce

1 mango, peeled and chopped
1 clove garlic, minced
2 tablespoons light corn syrup
1 tablespoon sweet chilli sauce

serves 4

i

preparation time
20 minutes

Cooking Time
25 minutes

nutritional value
fat: 3.8 g
carbohydrate: 5.7 g
protein: 14.6 g

1 Preheat barbecue to high.

2 Place chicken between sheets of wax paper and pound lightly with a meat mallet to flatten to ⅓ inch thick.

3 Combine black pepper, cumin and paprika and sprinkle over chicken. Layer prosciutto or ham and mango slices on chicken, roll up and secure with wooden toothpicks. Place chicken on lightly oiled barbecue and cook for 6–8 minutes each side or until chicken is tender and cooked.

4 In a small pan, place chopped mango, garlic, light corn syrup and sweet chilli sauce and cook, stirring, over a low heat for 4–5 minutes or until sauce thickens slightly. Serve with chicken.

barbecued chicken and mushroom patties

ingredients

500 g (1 lb) minced chicken
50 g (1³/₄ oz) dried breadcrumbs
1 onion, chopped
¹/₂ teaspoon salt
¹/₂ teaspoon pepper
2 tablespoons lemon juice
2 tablespoons chopped parsley
45 g (1¹/₂ oz) mushrooms,
  finely chopped
vegetable oil for cooking
makes 4-5 patties

i

preparation time
20 minutes

cooking time
20 minutes

nutritional value
fat: 12.6 g
carbohydrate: 5.1 g
protein: 13.3 g

1 Preheat barbecue to high. In a large bowl, place chicken, breadcrumbs, onion, salt, pepper, lemon juice, parsley and mushrooms. Mix well to combine, kneading with hands. With wet hands, shape into 4 or 5 large flat patties. Lightly oil barbecue grill bars.

2 Place patties on the barbecue and cook for 8 minutes on each side or until cooked through. Serve hot with vegetable accompaniments.

lemon barbecue roasted chicken with vegetables

ingredients

1 x 2 kg (4 lb) chicken
juice and grated zest of 2 lemons
2 cloves garlic, minced
salt and pepper
2 teaspoons chopped fresh oregano
2 tablespoons olive oil
4 potatoes, peeled and quartered
500 g (1 lb) pumpkin, unpeeled and
  cut into portions

serves 4-6

1 Wash chicken inside and out, drain then pat dry with paper towels. In a large bowl, place the lemon zest and juice, garlic, salt, pepper, oregano and oil and mix to combine.

2 Place chicken in a large pan and spoon half of the lemon mixture over the chicken and in the cavity.

3 Prepare kettle or hooded gas barbecue. Place chicken in barbecue.

4 Place potatoes and pumpkin in a large foil pan, sprinkle with remaining lemon mixture, tossing to coat. Place trays over direct heat. Cover barbecue with lid or hood and cook for 1–1½ hours, brushing chicken with lemon and herb mixture every 20 minutes. Turn vegetables.

5 Remove vegetables when cooked, cover to keep hot. Rest chicken for 5 minutes before carving. Serve hot with roasted vegetables and a side salad.

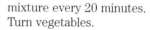

i

preparation time
25 minutes

cooking time
1½-2 hours

nutritional value
fat: 7.3 g
carbohydrate: 3.2 g
protein: 12.9 g

chicken and prosciutto roll-ups

ingredients

4 tablespoons dry white wine
2 teaspoons fresh thyme, finely chopped
4 (about 500 g, 1 lb) medium chicken
    breast fillet halves
4 thin slices prosciutto, trimmed of fat
60 g (2 oz) fontina cheese, thinly sliced
125 g (4 oz) roasted red bell pepper,
    cut into thin strips
extra fresh thyme to serve (optional)
serves 4

i

preparation time
35 minutes

cooking time
25 minutes

nutritional value
fat: 6.2 g
carbohydrate: 0.7 g
protein: 16.5 g

1 Preheat barbecue to medium. In a small bowl, combine wine and thyme, and set aside.

2 Pound each chicken fillet lightly with a meat mallet to about 2.5 mm thick, using plastic wrap to protect flesh.

3 Place a slice of prosciutto and ¼ of the cheese on each chicken fillet. Arrange ¼ of the roasted bell pepper on top near bottom edge of chicken. Starting from bottom edge, roll up and secure with wooden toothpicks.

Lightly oil barbecue grill bars. Place chicken on barbecue grill rack directly over heat for 15–17 minutes or until chicken is tender, turning to cook evenly and brushing occasionally with wine mixture. Garnish with additional fresh thyme, if desired.

deluxe chicken and roasted bell pepper sandwich

ingredients

4 tablespoons olive oil
4 teaspoons red-wine vinegar
1 tablespoon snipped fresh thyme
$1/2$ teaspoon salt
$1/4$ teaspoon paprika
4 (about 600 g, $1^1/4$ lb) chicken breast
   fillet halves
4 thick slices french or italian bread
60 g (2 oz) semi-soft cheese with herbs
   or semi-soft goat cheese (chevre)
250 g (8 oz) roasted red bell pepper,
   cut into strips
2 handfuls fresh watercress, basil, or
baby spinach leaves
makes 4

1 Preheat barbecue to high heat. In a small bowl beat together the oil, vinegar, thyme, salt and paprika, set aside. Reserve 2 tablespoons of the marinade. Place chicken between 2 sheets of wax paper, pound lightly with a meat mallet to about $1/3$ inch thick, place in a sealable plastic bag. Add the remaining

marinade. Seal bag and marinate for 15 minutes at room temperature or 1 hour in the refrigerator.

2 Lightly grease the barbecue grill racks. Brush bread with reserved marinade, place bread on barbecue – lightly toasting each side. Remove bread from barbecue, set aside.

3 Place chicken on the barbecue. Cook until chicken is tender, about 4–5 minutes each side. Remove from barbecue and spread or sprinkle with cheese.

4 To serve, place one chicken breast on each toasted bread slice. Top with roasted bell pepper strips and watercress.

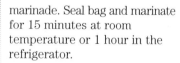

i

preparation time
30 minutes

cooking time
25 minutes

nutritional value
fat: 10.3 g
carbohydrate: 5.7 g
protein: 13.2 g

seafood

seared tuna with roasted plum tomatoes

ingredients

1 clove garlic, minced
finely grated zest and juice of 1 lime
$\frac{1}{2}$ cup (125 ml, 4 fl oz) olive oil
3 tablespoons chopped fresh rosemary
4 (145 g, 5 oz) tuna steaks,
    about $\frac{1}{2}$ inch thick
6 plum tomatoes, halved lengthways
1 red onion, halved and thinly sliced
    lengthways
salt and black pepper
extra olive oil for greasing
serves 4

1 Preheat barbecue to high. Preheat oven to 220°C (425°F, gas mark 7). In a large pan, combine garlic, lime zest, half the lime juice, 2 tablespoons of the oil and 1 tablespoon of the rosemary. Add the tuna and turn to coat evenly. Cover and refrigerate for 30 minutes.

2 Place the tomatoes and onion in a shallow ovenproof pan with the remaining rosemary. Drizzle with the remaining oil and season. Roast in the oven for 15–20 minutes, until tender and lightly browned.

3 Lightly oil barbecue grill bars. Place tuna on barbecue, cook for 4–5 minutes, turning once, or until golden. Serve with the tomatoes and onion, sprinkled with the remaining lime juice.

i

preparation time
20 minutes &
30 minutes
marinating

cooking time
30 minutes

nutritional value
fat: 21.6 g
carbohydrate: 1.7 g
protein: 5.1 g

home-smoked trout

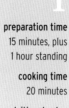

ingredients

125 g (4 oz) smoking chips
½ cup (125 ml, 4 fl oz) white wine
4 small rainbow trout, cleaned,
   with head and tail intact
1 tablespoon vegetable oil
3 red onions, thinly sliced
1 lemon, thinly sliced
8 sprigs dill

serves 4

i

preparation time
15 minutes, plus
1 hour standing

cooking time
20 minutes

nutritional value
fat: 4.8 g
carbohydrate: 0.9 g
protein: 19.4 g

1 Place smoking chips and wine in a large glass dish and stand for 1 hour.

2 Preheat covered barbecue to a low heat. Place smoking chips dish in barbecue over hot coals, cover barbecue with lid and heat for 5–10 minutes or until liquid is hot.

3 Place trout on a wire rack set in a roasting pan. Brush trout lightly with oil, then top with onions, lemon and dill. Place on rack in barbecue, cover and smoke for 15–20 minutes or until trout flakes when tested with fork.

char-grilled tuna with peach salsa

ingredients

4 (about 180 g, 6 oz) tuna steaks
1 tablespoon olive oil
cilantro
chopped to garnish
lime wedges to serve
salsa
3 ripe peaches, peeled, pitted and
   finely chopped
4 green onions, finely chopped
$1/2$ yellow bell pepper, finely chopped
juice of $1/2$ lime
1 tablespoon chopped cilantro
black pepper
serves 4

preparation time
20 minutes, plus
1 hour
refrigeration

cooking time
15 minutes

nutritional value
fat: 3.8 g
carbohydrate: 4.4 g
protein: 6.7 g

1 In a small bowl, place peaches, spring onions, bell pepper, lime juice, cilantro and black pepper and mix well. Cover and refrigerate for 1 hour.

2 Preheat the barbecue to high. Brush tuna steaks with oil and season with pepper. Place on barbecue and cook for 3–5 minutes on each side, until flesh flakes when tested with a fork. Garnish with cilantro and serve with the lime wedges and peach salsa.

seafood barbecue

ingredients

4 tablespoons soy sauce
2 tablespoons honey
2 tablespoons tomato sauce
2 tablespoons sesame seeds
1 tablespoon lemon zest,
    finely grated
375 g (12 oz) green shrimp, shelled and
    deveined, tails intact
250 g (8 oz) calamari (squid) rings
250 g (8 oz) boneless fish fillets,
    cut into thick strips
4 potatoes, thinly sliced
4 small tomatoes, halved
2 tablespoons chopped fresh thyme
freshly ground black pepper
lemon or lime wedges
serves 4

1 Preheat barbecue to a high heat. In a large shallow glass dish, place soy sauce, honey, tomato sauce, sesame seeds and lemon zest. Add shrimp, calamari and fish, toss to coat, cover and refrigerate for 20 minutes.

2 Sprinkle potatoes and tomatoes with thyme and black pepper to taste. Cook potatoes and tomatoes on a well-oiled barbecue plate for 10 minutes or until potatoes are crisp and tomatoes soft. Push vegetables to the side of the barbecue to keep warm.

3 Add seafood mixture to barbecue and cook, turning frequently, for 5 minutes or until cooked. Serve vegetables and seafood garnished with lemon or lime wedges.

i

preparation time
30 minutes, plus
20 minutes
marinating

cooking time
30 minutes

nutritional value
fat: 1.1 g
carbohydrate: 6.9 g
protein: 9.2 g

char-grilled baby octopus salad

ingredients

360 g (12 oz) baby octopus, cleaned
1 teaspoon sesame oil
1 tablespoon lime juice
4 tablespoons sweet chilli sauce
1 tablespoon fish sauce
60 g (2 oz) dried rice vermicelli
100 g (3½ oz) mixed salad leaves
90 g (3 oz) bean sprouts
1 lebanese cucumber, halved
200 g (6½ oz) cherry tomatoes, halved
2 handfuls cilantro
lime wedges, to serve

serves 4

1 Preheat barbecue to high. Rinse the cleaned octopus, pat dry with paper towel and place in a large glass bowl.

2 In a pitcher, place sesame oil, lime juice, sweet chilli

i

preparation time
20 minutes, plus
4 hours or
overnight
marinating

cooking time
10 minutes

nutritional value
fat: 1.3 g
carbohydrate: 4.2 g
protein: 8.7 g

sauce and fish sauce and beat to combine. Pour marinade over octopus, cover and marinade for 4 hours or overnight in the refrigerator. Drain and reserve the marinade.

3 In a large bowl, place vermicelli, cover with boiling water and allow to stand for 10 minutes or until soft. Drain well and set aside.

4 Divide the mixed salad leaves among four plates, top with bean sprouts, rice vermicelli, cucumber and tomato.

5 Cook octopus on a preheated barbecue about 4–5 minutes until tender and well colored. Place marinade in a small pan and bring to the boil. Serve octopus on top of salad, drizzle with hot marinade and garnish with cilantro and lime wedges.

lemon and herb-basted scallops

ingredients

4 tablespoons butter, melted
2 tablespoons lemon juice
1 clove garlic, minced
1 teaspoon finely chopped fresh basil
1 teaspoon finely chopped cilantro
1 teaspoon finely chopped fresh mint
500 g (1 lb) fresh scallops
1 red onion, cut into wedges
1 red bell pepper, cut into triangles
watercress for garnish
lemon wedges to serve
8-10 metal skewers
serves 6

1 Preheat barbecue plate to high. In a small bowl, combine the butter, lemon juice, garlic and herbs, and set aside.

2 Thread scallops, onion and bell pepper onto skewers, brushing each skewer with butter mixture.

3 Place skewers onto barbecue and cook for 4–5 minutes, turning once and brushing with remaining butter mixture, until scallops are tender. Serve garnished with watercress and lemon wedges.

i

preparation time
30 minutes

cooking time
15 minutes

nutritional value
fat: 8.3 g
carbohydrate: 1.8 g
protein: 7.7 g

bell pepper-barbecued whole snapper with gherkin mayonnaise relish

ingredients

1 whole snapper (1.5 kg, 3 lb)
3 tablespoons chopped red bell pepper
2 teaspoons chopped fresh basil
2 tablespoons lemon juice
1 tablespoon olive oil
gherkin mayonnaise
250 g (8 oz) mayonnaise
90 g (3 oz) gherkins, chopped
serves 4

1 Prepare kettle/weber for cooking or preheat barbecue to high. Cut and scale the fish and rinse well. Pat dry with paper towels.

2 In a small bowl, combine bell pepper, basil, lemon juice and oil. Spoon some into the cavity of the fish and spread the remainder over the

fish.

3 Lay the fish on a large sheet of oiled foil and roll up the edges to seal the fish,

leaving the top of the fish exposed. Place fish on the grill bars in kettle/weber or hooded gas barbecue and cook for 35–40 minutes or until fish flakes when tested with a fork.

If using a flat top, charcoal or gas barbecue cover the fish completely with foil. Place on a wire rack and place the rack on top of the grill bars, elevating so that the fish is 4 inches above the source of heat. Cook for 10–12 minutes each side. Turn carefully using a large spatula or place fish in a hinged fish rack and turn when needed.

4 In a small bowl, combine gherkin and mayonnaise. Serve mayonnaise in a separate dish.

i

preparation time
10-15 minutes

cooking time
25-40 minutes

nutritional value
fat: 6.3 g
carbohydrate: 3.5 g
protein: 15.8 g

lemon grass shrimp

ingredients

1 kg (2 lb) green shrimp
3 stalks fresh lemon grass,
   finely chopped
2 green onions, chopped
2 small fresh red chilli peppers,
   finely chopped
2 cloves garlic, minced
2 tablespoons finely grated fresh ginger
1 teaspoon shrimp paste
1 tablespoon light brown sugar
$\frac{1}{2}$ cup (125 ml, 4 fl oz) coconut milk

serves 4

i

preparation time
30 minutes, plus
3-4 hours
marinating

cooking time
15 minutes

nutritional value
fat: 2.7 g
carbohydrate: 1.7 g
protein: 17.4 g

1 Wash shrimp, leaving shells and heads intact and place in a shallow glass dish.

2 In a food processor or blender, place lemon grass, green onions, chillies, garlic, ginger and shrimp paste and process until smooth. Add sugar and coconut milk and process to combine. Spoon mixture over shrimp, toss to combine, cover and refrigerate for 3–4 hours.

3 Preheat barbecue to a high heat. Drain shrimp, place on barbecue and cook, tossing gently, for 3–5 minutes until cooked.

cilantro swordfish steaks

ingredients

125 g (4 oz) butter
2 tablespoons chopped cilantro
1 tablespoon parmesan, grated
4 swordfish steaks
1 tablespoon olive oil
4 small zucchini, cut into long slices
1 red bell pepper, quartered
serves 4

i

preparation time
20 minutes

cooking time
12 minutes

nutritional value
fat: 11.8 g
carbohydrate: 1.0 g
protein: 9.8 g

1 Preheat barbecue to high. Cream the butter until soft and add the cilantro and parmesan. Mix to combine, press into a butter pot and set aside.

2 Lightly oil barbecue grill bars. Brush fish steaks with oil, place on grill bars and cook 3–4 minutes each side according to thickness. Brush vegetables with oil and place

on grill, cook for 3–4 minutes until golden. Serve vegetables and swordfish topped with a dollop of cilantro butter.

vegetarian

barbecued vegetables

ingredients

300 g (10 oz) sweet potato, peeled and
cut into 1 inch thick slices
300 g (10 oz) squash, peeled and cut
into wedges
6 medium potatoes, halved
12 baby onions, whole
6 carrots, peeled
6 parsnips, peeled
6 baby beets, peeled
4 tablespoons olive oil
4 sprigs fresh thyme
4 sprigs fresh rosemary

serves 6

i

preparation time
20 minutes

cooking time
40 minutes

nutritional value
fat: 2.6 g
carbohydrate: 9.7 g
protein: 1.8 g

1 Preheat covered barbecue to a medium heat.

2 Bring a large pan of water to the boil, add sweet potato, squash and potatoes and cook for 10 minutes. Drain well.

3 Place sweet potato, squash, potatoes, onions, carrots, parsnips and beets on a lightly oiled baking pan. Brush vegetables lightly with oil and scatter with sprigs of thyme and rosemary.

4 Place baking pan on rack in barbecue, cover barbecue with lid and cook for 40 minutes or until vegetables are tender.

pesto potato wedges

ingredients

4 medium-sized potatoes, peeled
2 tablespoons basil pesto
1 tablespoon olive oil
1 tablespoon water
60 g (2 oz) parmesan, grated
serves 2-4

1 Preheat barbecue to high. Cut potatoes into wedges, rinse well and drain, then place in a large bowl. In a small bowl, combine basil pesto, olive oil and water. Pour over potatoes and toss to coat well. Place in a large foil pan in a single layer if possible.

2 Cook over indirect heat in a covered barbecue for 40 minutes, turning after 20 minutes.

3 Serve sprinkled with parmesan.

i

preparation time
15 minutes

cooking time
40 minutes

nutritional value
fat: 10.4 g
carbohydrate: 10.7 g
protein: 6.3 g

wild rice and bean patties

ingredients

440 g (14 oz) canned soya beans, drained and rinsed
6 tablespoons chopped cilantro
3 green onions, chopped
1 tablespoon finely grated fresh ginger
1 tablespoon ground cumin
1 tablespoon ground cilantro
½ teaspoon ground turmeric
½ cup (100 g, 3½ oz) wild rice blend, cooked
75 g (2½ oz) wholewheat flour
1 egg, lightly beaten
2 tablespoons vegetable oil

sweet chilli yogurt

1 cup (250 g, 8 oz) natural yogurt
2 tablespoons sweet chilli sauce
1 tablespoon lime juice

serves 6

i

preparation time
25 minutes

cooking time
10-15 minutes

nutritional value
fat: 7.2 g
carbohydrate: 9.4 g
protein: 6.6 g

1 Preheat barbecue to a medium heat. Into a food processor, place soya beans, cilantro, green onions, ginger, cumin, ground cilantro and turmeric and process for 30 seconds or until mixture resembles coarse breadcrumbs. Transfer mixture to a large bowl, add rice, flour and egg and mix to combine. Shape mixture into patties.

2 Heat oil on barbecue plate for 2–3 minutes or until hot, add patties and cook for 5 minutes each side or until golden and heated through.

3 In a small bowl, place yogurt, chilli sauce and lime juice and mix to combine. Serve with patties.

couscous-filled mushrooms

ingredients

$^2/_3$ cup (125 g, 4 oz) couscous
$^2/_3$ cup (170 ml, 5$^1/_2$ fl oz) boiling water
$^1/_2$ tablespoon butter
2 teaspoons olive oil
1 onion, chopped
2 cloves garlic, minced
1 teaspoon garam masala
pinch cayenne pepper
12 large mushrooms, stalks removed
200 g (7 oz) feta cheese, crumbled
serves 4

stirring, for 3 minutes or until onion is soft. Add garam masala and cayenne pepper and cook for a further minute. Add onion mixture to couscous and toss to combine.

minutes or until water is absorbed. Add butter and toss gently with a fork.

1 Preheat barbecue to a high heat. In a large bowl, place couscous, pour over boiling water, cover and set aside for 5

2 Heat oil in a large skillet over a medium heat, add onion and garlic and cook,

3 Fill mushrooms with couscous mixture, top with feta cheese and cook on lightly oiled barbecue grill for 5 minutes or until mushrooms are tender and cheese melts.

i

preparation time
20 minutes

cooking time
15 minutes

nutritional value
fat: 11.1 g
carbohydrate: 18.0 g
protein: 10.1 g

warm mushroom and leek salad

ingredients

2 tablespoons rice wine vinegar
1 shallot, chopped
2 teaspoons honey
1 teaspoon soy sauce
1 clove garlic, minced
¹/₂ teaspoon toasted sesame oil
¹/₄ teaspoon white pepper
3 tablespoons vegetable oil
3 leeks
200 g (7oz) shiitake mushrooms
300 g (10oz) button mushrooms
250 g (7oz) field mushrooms
1 tablespoon sesame seeds, toasted
makes 6 side-dish servings

preparation time
20 minutes

cooking time
30 minutes

nutritional value
fat: 5.9 g
carbohydrate: 3.0 g
protein: 3.1 g

1 Preheat barbecue to medium heat. In a food processor or blender combine rice-wine vinegar, shallot, honey, soy sauce, garlic, sesame oil and white pepper. With machine running, slowly add canola oil, process until smooth and set aside.

2 Trim roots and green leaves from leeks. In a large pan cook leeks in boiling water for about 8 minutes or until just tender, drain and halve lengthwise. Insert a wooden toothpick through one end of each leek to hold it together while barbecuing. Remove and discard stems from mushrooms. Rinse mushroom caps, pat dry with paper towels.

3 Place leeks and mushrooms on flat barbecue plate directly over heat. Cook for 5–8 minutes or until tender, tossing gently. Remove from barbecue, cool slightly and coarsely chop.

4 In a large serving bowl, toss the vegetables with dressing. If desired, serve the vegetable mixture on lettuce leaves. Sprinkle with sesame seeds.

cajun barbecue corn

ingredients

4 cobs sweet corn, halved
1 orange sweet potato, cut into
  $1/3$ inch thick slices
2 tablespoons butter, melted
cajun spice mix
1 teaspoon freshly ground black pepper
$1/2$ teaspoon chilli powder
1 teaspoon ground cumin
1 teaspoon ground cilantro
2 teaspoons sweet paprika
serves 4

1 Preheat barbecue to a high heat.

2 In a small bowl, place black pepper, chilli powder, cumin, cilantro and paprika and mix to combine.

3 Brush sweet corn and sweet potato with butter, sprinkle spice mix over vegetables. Place sweet corn and sweet potato on barbecue and cook, turning frequently, for 10–15 minutes or until vegetables are almost cooked.

i

preparation time
15 minutes

cooking time
25 minutes

nutritional value
fat: 4.7 g
carbohydrate: 15.2 g
protein: 3.6 g

glossary

al dente: Italian term to describe pasta and rice that are cooked until tender but still firm to the bite.

bake blind: to bake pastry cases without their fillings. Line the raw pastry case with wax paper and fill with raw rice or dried beans to prevent collapsed sides and puffed base. Remove paper and fill 5 minutes before completion of cooking time.

baste: to spoon hot cooking liquid over food at intervals during cooking to moisten and flavor it.

beat: to make a mixture smooth with rapid and regular motions using a spatula, wire whisk or electric mixer; to make a mixture light and smooth by enclosing air.

beurre manié: equal quantities of butter and flour mixed together to a smooth paste and stirred little by little into a soup, stew or sauce while on the heat to thicken. Stop adding when desired thickness results.

bind: to add egg or a thick sauce to hold ingredients together when cooked.

blanch: to plunge some foods into boiling water for less than a minute and immediately plunge into iced water. This is to brighten the color of some vegetables; to remove skin from tomatoes and nuts.

blend: to mix 2 or more ingredients thoroughly together; do not confuse with blending in an electric blender.

boil: to cook in a liquid brought to boiling point and kept there.

boiling point: when bubbles rise continually and break over the entire surface of the liquid, reaching a temperature of 100°C (212°F). In some cases food is held at this high temperature for a few seconds then heat is turned to low for slower cooking. See simmer.

bouquet garni: a bundle of several herbs tied together with string for easy removal, placed into pots of stock, soups and stews for flavor. A few sprigs of fresh thyme, parsley and bay leaf are used. Can be purchased in sachet form for convenience.

caramelize: to heat sugar in a heavy pan until it liquefies and develops a caramel color. Vegetables such as blanched carrots and sautéed onions may be sprinkled with sugar and caramelized.

chill: to place in the refrigerator or stir over ice until cold.

clarify: to make a liquid clear by removing sediments and impurities. To melt fat and remove any sediment.

coat: to dust or roll food items in flour to cover the surface before the food is cooked. Also, to coat in flour, egg and breadcrumbs.

cool: to stand at room temperature until some or all heat is removed, e.g., cool a little, cool completely.

cream: to make creamy and fluffy by working the mixture with the back of a wooden spoon, usually refers to creaming butter and sugar or margarine. May also be creamed with an electric mixer.

croutons: small cubes of bread, toasted or fried, used as an addition to salads or as a garnish to soups and stews.

crudite: raw vegetable sticks served with a dipping sauce.

crumb: to coat foods in flour, egg and breadcrumbs to form a protective coating for foods that are fried. Also adds flavor, texture and enhances appearance.

cube: to cut into small pieces with six even sides, e.g., cubes of meat.

cut in: to combine fat and flour using 2 knives scissor fashion or with a pastry blender, to make pastry.

deglaze: to dissolve dried out cooking juices left on the bottom and sides of a roasting dish or skillet. Add a little water, wine or stock, scrape and stir over heat until dissolved. Resulting liquid is used to make a flavorsome gravy or added to a sauce or casserole.

degrease: to skim fat from the surface of cooking liquids, e.g., stocks, soups, casseroles.

dice: to cut into small cubes.

dredge: to heavily coat with powdered sugar, sugar, flour or cornstarch.

dressing: a mixture added to completed dishes to add moisture and flavor, e.g., salads, cooked vegetables.

drizzle: to pour in a fine thread-like stream moving over a surface.

egg wash: beaten egg with milk or water used to brush over pastry, bread dough or cookies to give a sheen and golden brown color.

essence: a strong flavoring liquid, usually made by distillation. Only a few drops are needed to flavor.

fillet: a piece of prime meat, fish or poultry that is boneless or has all bones removed.

flake: to separate cooked fish into flakes, removing any bones and skin, using 2 forks.

flame: to ignite warmed alcohol over food or to pour into a pan with food, ignite then serve.

flute: to make decorative indentations around the pastry edge before baking.

fold in: combining of a light, whipped or creamed mixture with other ingredients. Add a portion of the other ingredients at a time and mix using a gentle circular motion, over and under the mixture so that air will not be lost. Use a silver spoon or spatula.

glaze: to brush or coat food with a liquid that will give the finished product a glossy appearance, and on baked products, a golden brown color.

grease: to rub the surface of a metal or heatproof dish with oil or fat, to prevent the food from sticking.

herbed butter: softened butter mixed with finely chopped fresh herbs and re-chilled. Used to serve on grilled meats and fish.

hors d'ouvre: small savory foods served as an appetizer, popularly known today as "finger food".

infuse: to steep foods in a liquid until the liquid absorbs their flavor.

joint: to cut poultry and game into serving pieces by dividing at the joint.

julienne: to cut some food, e.g., vegetables and processed meats into fine strips the length of matchsticks. Used for inclusion in salads or as a garnish to cooked dishes.

knead: to work a yeast dough in a pressing, stretching and folding motion with the heel of the hand until smooth and elastic to develop the gluten strands. Non-yeast doughs should be lightly and quickly handled as gluten development is not desired.

line: to cover the inside of a baking pan with paper for the easy removal of the cooked product from the baking pan.

macerate: to stand fruit in a syrup, liqueur or spirit to give added flavor.

marinade: a flavored liquid, into which food is placed for some time to give it flavor and to tenderize. Marinades include an acid ingredient such as vinegar or wine, oil and seasonings.

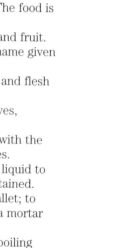

mask: to evenly cover cooked food portions with a sauce, mayonnaise or savory jelly.

pan-fry: to fry foods in a small amount of fat or oil, sufficient to coat the bottom of the pan.

parboil: to boil until partially cooked. The food is then finished by some other method.

pare: to peel the skin from vegetables and fruit. Peel is the popular term but pare is the name given to the knife used; paring knife.

pith: the white lining between the rind and flesh of oranges, grapefruit and lemons.

pit: to remove stones or seeds from olives, cherries, dates.

pitted: the olives, cherries, dates, etc., with the stone removed, e.g., purchase pitted dates.

poach: to simmer gently in enough hot liquid to almost cover the food so shape will be retained.

pound: to flatten meats with a meat mallet; to reduce to a paste or small particles with a mortar and pestle.

simmer: to cook in liquid just below boiling point at about 96°C (205°F) with small bubbles rising gently to the surface.

skim: to remove fat or froth from the surface of simmering food.

stock: the liquid produced when meat, poultry, fish or vegetables have been simmered in water to extract the flavor. Used as a base for soups, sauces, casseroles, etc. Convenience stock products are available.

sweat: to cook sliced onions or vegetables, in a small amount of butter in a covered pan over low heat, to soften them and release flavor without coloring.

conversions

measurements differ from country to country, so it's important to understand what the differences are. This Measurements Guide gives you simple "at-a-glance" information for using the recipes in this book, wherever you may be.

Cooking is not an exact science – minor variations in measurements won't make a difference to your cooking.

equipment

There is a difference in the size of measuring cups used internationally, but the difference is minimal (only 2–3 teaspoons). We use the Australian standard metric measurements in our recipes:

1 teaspoon ....5 ml	1 tablespoon....20 ml
½ cup......125 ml	1 cup.....250 ml
4 cups...1 liter	

Measuring cups come in sets of one cup (250 ml), ½ cup (125 ml), ⅓ cup (80 ml) and ¼ cup (60 ml). Use these for measuring liquids and certain dry ingredients.
Measuring spoons come in a set of four and should be used for measuring dry and liquid ingredients.
When using cup or spoon measures always make them level (unless the recipe indicates otherwise).

dry versus wet ingredients

While this system of measures is consistent for liquids, it's more difficult to quantify dry ingredients. For instance, one level cup equals: 200 g of brown sugar; 210 g of superfine sugar; and 110 g of powdered sugar.

When measuring dry ingredients such as flour, don't push the flour down or shake it into the cup. It is best just to spoon the flour in until it reaches the desired amount. When measuring liquids use a clear vessel indicating metric levels.

Always use medium eggs (1.5-2.5 oz) when eggs are required in a recipe.

dry

metric (grams)	imperial (ounces)
30 g	1 oz
60 g	2 oz
90 g	3 oz
100 g	3½ oz
125 g	4 oz
150 g	5 oz
185 g	6 oz
200 g	7 oz
250 g	8 oz
280 g	9 oz
315 g	10 oz
330 g	11 oz
370 g	12 oz
400 g	13 oz
440 g	14 oz
470 g	15 oz
500 g	16 oz (1 lb)
750 g	24 oz (1½ lb)
1000 g (1 kg)	32 oz (2 lb)

liquids

metric (milliliters)	imperial (fluid ounces)
30 ml	1 fl oz
60 ml	2 fl oz
90 ml	3 fl oz
100 ml	3½ fl oz
125 ml	4 fl oz
150 ml	5 fl oz
190 ml	6 fl oz
250 ml	8 fl oz
300 ml	10 fl oz
500 ml	16 fl oz
600 ml	20 fl oz (1 pint)*
1000 ml (1 liter)	32 fl oz

*Note: an American pint is 16 fl oz.

oven
Your oven should always be at the right temperature before placing the food in it to be cooked. Note that if your oven doesn't have a fan you may need to cook food for a little longer.

microwave
It is difficult to give an exact cooking time for microwave cooking. It is best to watch what you are cooking closely to monitor its progress.

standing time
Many foods continue to cook when you take them out of the oven or microwave. If a recipe states that the food needs to "stand" after cooking, be sure not to overcook the dish.

can sizes
The can sizes available in your supermarket or grocery store may not be the same as specified in the recipe. Don't worry if there is a small variation in size—it's unlikely to make a difference to the end result.

cooking temperatures	°C (celsius)	°F (fahrenheit)	gas mark
very slow	120	250	1/2
slow	150	300	2
moderately slow	160	315	2-3
moderate	180	350	4
moderate hot	190	375	5
	200	400	6
hot	220	425	7
very hot	230	450	8
	240	475	9
	250	500	10

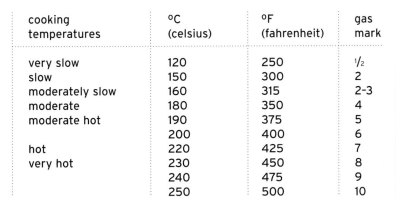

index